Barrilete

A Kite for the Day of the Dead

Elisa Amado

Photographs by **Joya Hairs**

A Groundwood Book   Douglas & McIntyre   Toronto   Vancouver   Buffalo

The rainy season is coming to an end. When Juan looks up at the sky, he sees fewer fluffy white clouds blowing up the valley on the soft south wind. The corn, *la milpa*, that feeds his village, is almost ready to harvest.

Now is the time to get ready for the most important day of the year.

El Día de los Muertos, the
Day of the Dead, is also the
day of the kites, *los barriletes*,
in Santiago Sacatepéquez,
where Juan lives with his
parents and his brothers, José
and Beto.

Abuelo, their grandfather, used to make the kite with the boys' help. But this year Abuelo died just before the rains, *las lluvias*, came — just when *la milpa* was poking up out of the steep hillside fields. Now Juan must try to remember all the things Abuelo taught him. With the help of José and his friends, Tomás and Rafa, he will build the kite himself. Beto is very little, but he will learn by helping as they once did.

The little boys of Santiago
climb onto their roofs and test
the wind with small kites. They
are impatient.

The leaves of *la milpa* shine golden in the sun. The corn is ready to be picked. And then one day Juan notices that some of the village fields have been harvested and cleared. It is getting cooler. This morning José told him he could see his breath when he went out to wash his face in *la pila*, the basin in the yard behind his house.

Now the boys have time to go to market. When they come home, they are carrying a pile of *papel de china*. The tissue paper is red, yellow, blue, green and orange — like a rainbow, *un arco iris*.

The paper is cut into squares, triangles and rectangles. First a cardboard circle is cut for the center. Then round and round, piece by piece, the bright paper is pasted in an ever growing circle. Inside the dark house the colors glow softly.

This is the best time of all. Each kite in Santiago will be different. Some people will put pictures on their kites, others just plain patterns.

Other boys and girls of the village, the grown-ups, too, are all busy preparing for the day. Time to go and see how other families are getting along. How big will Rosa's brother's kite be? Hasn't Juanita's family even started yet? They'll never be ready!

Once the kites are up in the air, they will rip a little, but no one min
because they are still beautiful.

Beto likes to fly little kites. It is easier.

Today Juan's mother is making tortillas from the new corn. Last night she ground the corn on her stone *metate*. She added water and lime, then let it sit overnight. Juan can hear the sound of her hands *torteando*, slapping a ball of *masa*, dough, into the shape of a circle and then down onto *el comal*, a flat clay plate sitting on the fire. A delicious smell fills the house. Beto loves tortillas and eats as many as he can. A neighbor helps him.

When Juan walks outside, he can see that the *Volcan de Fuego* has been erupting. It often does. But instead of rising straight up into the sky, the plume of smoke is bending. *Está norteando.* The north wind is blowing. The sky overhead is deep blue. It is getting ready for *el Día de los Muertos*, too.

Everything is ready. It is almost time. The kite is lying folded on the floor. Sticks for building the frame, made from the wild reed, *caña brava*, are stacked in the yard of the house, waiting to be attached to the kite.

First comes *Todos Santos*, All Saints' Day. Juan and José stay home while their family goes to Mass. Many people in the village are there. The church is smoky from the candles and *el copal*, incense, burning in front of the altar. But Juan and José and their friends are busy getting ready for tomorrow.

They lay the great circle of paper on the ground. Then they place the spokes inside, just so. If they are too far apart, the paper will tear. If they are too close together, the kite will be too heavy.

While they work, they remember everything Abuelo taught them. They remember how the old man's strong hands tied and cut and pasted paper to make the most beautiful *barrilete* in the world, and how he mounted it onto the frame to make it steady.

A string is tied around *las cañas* almost at their ends to create a big circle. The colored paper circle is folded over the string and glued in place. Finally, three ropes are tied onto *las cañas* right through the paper and attached to the flying rope itself.

Now they make the fringe, which rustles when the wind is strong enough to lift the kite. They can't decide whether to add flags to their kite, as many people do. In the end they do.

Just as the sky turns morning pink over the mountains, Juan runs outside. The dew has frozen on the grass. It is cold but there is no wind. He runs back inside. It is time to get ready, time to go. But where is the wind?

Soon the whole village is up. Huge kites are carried down the small village roads between the adobe walls of the houses, down to *el cementerio*.

People are buried here, some in what look like small houses. On *el Día de los Muertos* the village comes to *el cementerio* to sit with the dead and keep them company. They pray for them and tell them what has been happening in the village all year.

Juan whispers to Abuelo. "Today I will fly the kite I made for you. I hope you like it. I hope it flies."

Just then Juan shivers a little. He looks up. A gust of cold wind has tickled his neck. As the sun rises in the sky, the wind grows stronger. He can see pine needles move. He can see his kite and all the kites trembling a little. He can hear the fringe rustling.

The time has come. Tomás, Rafa and José run over. They pick up the huge kite. Beto watches. He wishes he were bigger.

Juan takes the heavy ball of rope. Will it work? Will it fly?

All around him, people are doing the same. The kites are straining at the wind.

Juan gathers up his rope and starts to run down the hill. He can feel the kite pulling. "Abuelo," he prays, "make my kite fly. It will fly for you."

And then suddenly he feels a lift on the other end of the line. He looks over his shoulder, and there *el barrilete* is just leaving José's hand on its way up to the sky.

Rafa runs over to help.
Juan digs his heels into the
ground as the kite almost pulls
him off his feet. More line and
up it flies, higher and higher.
The sky is full of color as the
kites of Santiago swoop over
el cementerio.

Juan can feel the wind in his hair and the kite's flight in his hand. Abuelo must be up there soaring and dipping and turning, looking down on his village and on Juan and José, his grandsons, and on Beto, too, flying the beautiful *barrilete* they have made.

In Guatemala, there is a village called Santiago Sacatepéquez. It is a very small village but a famous one, nonetheless, because once a year on November 2, the Day of the Dead, the people of Santiago fly some of the biggest kites in the world. The kites can be as big as seven meters (twenty-three feet) in diameter and are all made by hand by the people of the village.

The people who live in Santiago are Quiché Maya, descended from one of the greatest civilizations ever known. Among other things, the Maya were great artists who painted brilliantly colored murals and books. Their descendants, who still live in Guatemala and Mexico, are known for the beauty of their handicrafts and weaving. The kites of Santiago, with elaborate designs of brilliantly colored paper, are another form of art made by the Maya today.

Barrilete is the Guatemalan word for kite. The same word is used in Argentina. But there are almost as many different names for kite in Latin America as there are countries. In Bolivia and Chile it is called *volantín*; in Brazil and Paraguay *pandorga*. Colombians, Cubans, Ecuadorans, Panamanians, Peruvians and people in Uruguay call it *cometa*, as do Spaniards. But in Salvador and Nicaragua a kite is *piscucha*, in Honduras *papelote*, while in Mexico it is called *papalote*, which is a Nahuatl (Aztec) word for butterfly. In Puerto Rico the very same kite is called a *chiringa*, but in the Dominican Republic it is a *chichigua*, while in Venezuela you fly a *papagayo*.

Groundwood Books/Douglas & McIntyre
585 Bloor Street West
Toronto, Ontario M6G 1K5

Distributed in the USA by Publishers Group West
1700 Fourth Street
Berkeley, CA 94710

We acknowledge the financial support of the Canada Council
for the Arts, the Ontario Arts Council and the Government of
Canada through the Book Publishing Industry Development
Program for our publishing activities.

Canadä

Canadian Cataloguing in Publication Data
Amado, Elisa
Barrilete : a kite for the Day of the Dead
A Groundwood book.
ISBN 0-88899-366-8
I. Hairs, Joya. II. Title.
PS8551.M33B37 1999   jC813'.54   C99-932006-8
PZ7.A4913Ba 1999

Design by Michael Solomon
Printed and bound in China
by Everbest Printing Co. Ltd.